THE STORY OF CHOCOLATE

First published in 2016 by Wayland
© Wayland 2016

Written by Alex Woolf
Cover illustration by Donough O'Malley
Designer: Balley Design Limited

A catalogue for this title is
available from the British Library

ISBN: 978 0 7502 9659 5

10 9 8 7 6 5 4 3 2 1

MIX
Paper from
responsible sources
FSC® C104740

Wayland
An imprint of
Hachette Children's Books
Part of Hodder & Stoughton
Carmelite House
50 Victoria Embankment
London, EC4Y 0DZ

An Hachette UK Company
www.hachette.co.uk
www.hachettechildrens.co.uk

Printed in China

Picture credits: Picture credits: p4 © omphoto/Shutterstock; p5 © Ammit Jack/
Shutterstock; p6 © Robert B. Goodman/Getty Images; p7 © mosista/Shutterstock;
p7 © Olesia Bilkei/Shutterstock; p8 © Mila Supinskaya/Shutterstock; p9 © Deyan
Georgiev/Shutterstock (t); p9 © Darrin Jenkins / Alamy Stock Photo (b); p10 © National
Geographic Creative/Corbis; p11 © Enrique Perez Huerta/Demotix/Corbis; p12 © Everett
Historical/Shutterstock; p13 © Everett Historical/Shutterstock; p14 © Roger-Viollet/REX
Shutterstock; p15 © Roger-Viollet/REX Shutterstock (t); p15 © PRISMA ARCHIVO/Alamy
Stock Photo (b); p16 © Shaiith/Shutterstock; p17 © Hulton-Deutsch Collection/Corbis;
p18 © Oldtime/Alamy Stock Photo; p19 ©Leemage/Corbis; p20 © Heritage Images/
Getty Images; p21 © Swim Ink 2, LLC/Corbis; p22 © Pictorial Press Ltd/Alamy Stock
Photo; p23 © Tony Evans/Timelapse Library Ltd./Getty Images; p23 © Amoret Tanner/
Alamy Stock Photo; p24 © Apic /Getty Images; p25 © gcpics/Shutterstock; p25 © s74/
Shutterstock; p26 © Bettmann/Corbis; p27 © dcwcreations/Shutterstock; p27 © Charles
Phelps Cushing/ClassicStock/Corbis; p28 © Maya Kruchankova/Shutterstock; p29 ©
Olivier Asselin/Alamy Stock Photo. Background images and other graphic elements
courtesy of Shutterstock.com.

CONTENTS

WHAT IS CHOCOLATE?

It can take the form of a solid bar, or a coating for other sweet things. It can be a creamy filling for a cake, a flavour of ice cream or a warm, sweet drink. It can vary in colour from white to dark brown and it can be creamy or crumbly. It's certainly delicious! But what exactly *is* chocolate? Where does it come from and how is it made? In this book we'll explore the answers to all these questions. We'll peel away the foil wrapping to reveal some of the bittersweet secrets of this fascinating food.

We usually think of chocolate as a solid bar, but for much of its history, it was drunk, not eaten.

WHAT'S IT MADE OF?

What we think of as chocolate – that delicious brown sweet stuff – is a product made up of many different ingredients. These include sugar, lecithin (a substance that smooths, blends and thickens ingredients), vanilla and other flavours, and often milk. But the core ingredient – the thing that makes chocolate different from every other sweet and tasty thing out there – is the cocoa bean. That is the seed of the fruit of the cacao tree.

A LONG HISTORY

Chocolate was first made thousands of years ago by farmers in Central America. They used cocoa beans to make a bitter drink. It was discovered by Spanish conquerors who came to the Americas in the 16th century and brought it back to Europe. The Spanish added sugar and honey, and it soon became a favourite among Europe's wealthy upper classes. Cacao *plantations* spread through the European *colonies* in the New World (the Americas) to satisfy demand, and slaves were brought over from Africa to work on these.

Over the centuries that followed, European sweet makers started mixing it with new ingredients to make it smoother, sweeter and creamier. It remained an elite treat until the *Industrial Revolution* in Europe and America, when steam-powered machines speeded up the processing of the cocoa bean. In the 19th century, the drink became a food with the arrival of the chocolate bar. Soon afterwards, milk chocolate was invented.

These 'pods' are the fruit of the cacao tree. Inside the pods are the cocoa beans.

CACAO OR COCOA?

The two words seem very similar, so what's the difference between them? Well that depends on where you live. **Cacao** is the name of the tree – everyone agrees on that. The British call the tree's seeds **cocoa** beans, and use the word **cocoa** for all the products of those beans, such as cocoa powder and cocoa butter. Americans call them **cacao** beans, and use the word **cacao** for the raw, unprocessed products. Once the beans have been processed, Americans call them and their products cocoa. In this book, we'll be following British usage.

CACAO FARMING

Cacao trees flourish in hot, rainy, tropical climates, and are mainly grown in areas close to the *equator*, such as West Africa, Southeast Asia and Central and South America. The scientific name of the trees is *Theobroma cacao*. The cacao fruit is called a pod and the seeds of the pod are the cocoa beans. The trees start producing cocoa beans by their third or fourth year, and can live for more than 200 years. However, trees more than 25 years old rarely produce usable cocoa beans.

FRAGILE TREES

Cacao trees are delicate and difficult to grow. In the wild, they live beneath taller trees in rainforests, which shelter them from the wind and sun. For this reason, they are often farmed alongside taller rubber and fruit trees that can give them shade.

Because they are so fragile, cacao trees are vulnerable to pests and diseases. Farmers must continually cut off sickly pods. Another threat farmers face is from squirrels, monkeys and rats that steal the pods for their tasty white pulp (though they ignore the bitter-tasting seeds themselves). Because of these problems, farmers lose, on average, 30 per cent of their crop each year.

The pods are harvested from the tree's trunk and major branches.

Inside each pod is a
sweet, juicy pulp that
covers the cocoa beans.

HARVESTING THE BEANS

Pods ripen after five to six months. Inside the pod is a sweet, white pulp and the beans – 50 or 60 in each pod. Harvest takes place twice a year in spring and autumn. Each tree produces around 2,500 beans per harvest. Workers pick the beans by hand using a mallet, *machete* or knife to slice off the ripened yellow-orange pods.

After gathering, the pods are split, and the seeds and pulp are scooped out. The seeds are raked into heaps and covered with banana leaves. As they *ferment*, they become less bitter and start to give off a chocolatey smell. After two to eight days, they change from purple to rich brown. They're placed on mats and sun-dried to make them transportable. Then they're put in sacks and sent to chocolate factories around the world.

VARIETIES

There are three main varieties of cacao tree:
Criollo: Known as the 'prince of cacaos', this is a rare, expensive variety, grown mainly in Central America and the Caribbean. It produces beans with a subtle, delicate, complex taste. Only 5 per cent of the world's chocolate comes from criollo.
Forastero: The most commonly grown variety, it flourishes in Brazil and Africa, and is much easier to grow than criollo. The flavour is described as 'classic chocolate', but also 'quite bland'.
Trinitario: A *hybrid* of criollo and forastero, trinitario originated in Trinidad, but is now found in many other places. It produces a smooth, rich-flavoured chocolate.

Cacao pods come in a variety of colours and sizes.

MOVABLE LEAVES

Cacao leaves can move 90 degrees, from horizontal to vertical, to catch the sun and protect younger leaves.

FROM BEANS TO CHOCOLATE

When they arrive at the factory, the chocolate makers inspect and approve the beans. If necessary, they will blend them with others from different regions to ensure the flavour is always the same. The beans are cleaned, then loaded into large cylinders for roasting.

Workers select the best quality cocoa beans when they arrive at the factory.

MAKING PURE CHOCOLATE

The beans are roasted for 30 to 120 minutes at 121°C. During this time, their brown colour deepens and the chocolate smell gets stronger. Once roasted, the beans are sent through a machine called a 'cracker and fanner' that splits their shells and blows them away from the 'meat' inside, called the 'nib'. The nibs are then ground in mills to create chocolate liquor (here meaning 'liquid'), which is poured into moulds that harden to form plain, unsweetened chocolate, also known as cooking chocolate.

PRESSURE

Modern presses weigh up to 25 tonnes and produce so much pressure that the cocoa butter, the natural fat inside of cocoa beans, melts.

MAKING EATING CHOCOLATE

The unsweetened chocolate is pumped into giant presses that squeeze the chocolate until it separates into cocoa butter (a yellow, fatty liquid) and a dry brown cake that is ground to produce cocoa powder. Cocoa butter is what gives chocolate that melt-in-your-mouth quality.

To make eating chocolate, chocolate liquor is mixed with sugar, cocoa butter, lecithin and vanilla, then stirred, melted and ground into a smooth paste. Milk or milk powder is added to make white or milk chocolate. White chocolate does not contain chocolate liquor.

Chocolate being conched so it's really smooth.

CONCHING AND TEMPERING

A 'conching' machine kneads the chocolate paste for hours or even days, stirring it. This removes the grittiness and makes it smoother. The more expensive types of chocolate are conched for up to three days, compared to four to six hours for mass-produced chocolate.

The chocolate is then tempered – stirred while heated, then cooled and reheated. This process evens out the *crystallisation* of the cocoa butter and makes the chocolate harder and glossier. Untempered chocolate tends to be dull-coloured with a crumbly texture.

A waterfall of warm chocolate is poured over handmade treats.

THE FINAL STAGE

Finally, the chocolate is poured into moulds or over other ingredients such as nougat, caramel, cream or nuts, to create the delicious chocolates that are sold in shops. To do this, the centres are placed on a wire conveyor belt and passed under a thin waterfall of warm chocolate. The final products go to a cooling chamber before being packaged.

THE ORIGINS OF CHOCOLATE

The story of chocolate began around 4,000 years ago in the area now known as southern Mexico. This is where cacao trees were first cultivated for their seeds. The earliest evidence found of chocolate being consumed is the *residue* of some cocoa left in a bowl, dating from 1900 BCE.

OLMECS

The Olmecs were a group of Central American people who flourished from 1600 to 100 BCE. They made a bitter drink from ground cocoa nibs mixed with water, which they called *kakaw*. It was used for religious rituals and perhaps as a medicine. They drank it cold or hot and added flavourings such as allspice, cinnamon, chilli powder and vanilla. They may even have mixed in maize, or sweetened it with honey or syrup from agave or cactus. They made it frothy by shaking it or pouring it from a height, then drank the foam.

The Olmecs were the first people we know of to make chocolate from cocoa beans.

This Mayan carving shows Ek Ahau, god of merchants and cacao-growers, next to a cacao tree.

MAYA

The Mayas were another group of Central American people and they described chocolate as 'the food of the gods'. They included images of the pods on their stone sculptures and there are images of the cacao tree and the chocolate drink in Mayan art, and in their sacred book, the *Popol Vuh*. They planted cacao trees in their gardens and made special cups or bowls for drinking the chocolate from. The Maya used chocolate in royal and religious ceremonies and at weddings. The Mayans traded chocolate with people from far and wide. They packed the cocoa with cornmeal and shaped it into small, round slabs to create a convenient snack for their warriors to eat while on the march.

AZTECS

Cacao trees would not grow in the dry highlands of central Mexico where the Aztecs (see page 13) lived, so they had to *import* it. They would demand that conquered peoples living in cacao-growing areas pay them *tribute* in the form of cocoa beans. The beans were so highly valued that they were even used as money.

The Aztecs believed that the cacao tree was a gift from their god named Quetzalcoatl. According to their myths, he had been banished from paradise by the other gods for sharing this sacred drink with humans. Priests made cocoa bean offerings to Quetzalcoatl and other gods.

ORIGIN OF THE WORD

Some scholars believe the word *chocolate* comes from the Aztec word *chocolatl*. Others say that this was a word the Spanish created by combining the Aztec word *cacahuatl* ('bitter water') with the Mayan word *chocol haa* ('hot water').

THE
SPANISH DISCOVER CHOCOLATE

In 1492, the Italian explorer Christopher Columbus arrived in the Caribbean, marking the beginning of the European discovery and colonisation of the Americas. On Columbus's fourth visit to the Caribbean, in 1502, he landed on the island of Guanaja, some 50 km north of Honduras, and it was here that he and his men became the first Europeans to encounter the cocoa bean.

Columbus was one of the first Europeans to encounter the cocoa bean.

MYSTERY BEANS

On 15 August, Columbus and his men captured a large Mayan trading canoe. On board, they found cocoa beans but they mistook them for almonds. Columbus's son Ferdinand noted how much the natives valued the beans: 'They seemed to hold these almonds at a great price … I observed that when any … fell, they all stooped to pick it up, as if an eye had fallen.'

A DRINK FOR A KING

It was reported that the Aztec court of King Montezuma drank 2,000 cups of chocolate a day, 50 of which were drunk by the king himself.

CONQUISTADORS

In 1519, Spanish *conquistadors*, led by Hernán Cortés, arrived in Mexico and confronted the greatest *Mesoamerican* power, the Aztecs. The conquistadors were at first welcomed at the court of the Aztec ruler Montezuma, where they were served chocolate. In 1521, the conquistadors defeated the Aztecs in battle. As the new masters of Mexico, the Spanish demanded that the Aztecs hand over their treasures, including their stocks of cocoa. Sensing its value, the conquistadors began to demand cocoa from the same peoples who had formerly offered it to the Aztecs as tribute.

NEW METHODS

The Spanish soon mastered the chocolate-making skills of the natives. They used some of the traditional methods, such as grinding the shelled beans on a heated 'metate' – a curved grinding stone – but also introduced new techniques. For example, while the Aztecs created froth by pouring the chocolate from a height, the Spanish whipped the hot chocolate into a smooth foam by beating it with a large wooden stick called a 'molinillo'. The Spanish also discovered a way of making an instant chocolate drink from a wafer of dried, ground cocoa simply by adding hot water and sugar. These wafers turned out to be a handy way of storing and moving cocoa.

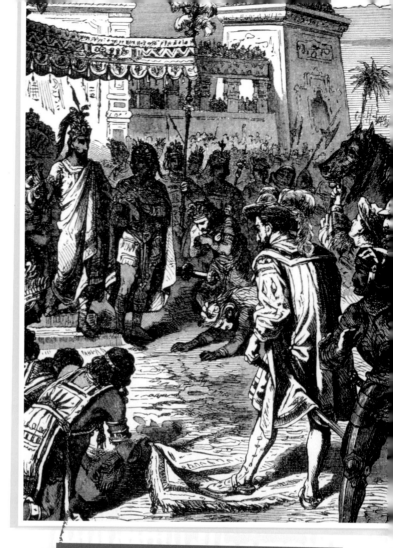

Hernán Cortés, leader of the Spanish conquistadors, meets Aztec ruler Montezuma.

A SCUM-LIKE BUBBLING ...

In 1590, Jose de Acosta, a Spanish *Jesuit missionary*, wrote: 'The main benefit of this cacao is a beverage which they make called Chocolate ... It disgusts those who are not used to it, for it has a foam on top, or a scum-like bubbling ... And the Spanish men – and even more the Spanish women – are addicted to the black chocolate.'

CHOCOLATE COMES TO EUROPE

Chocolate was introduced to Spain in 1544. That year, a group of men returned to Spain with some Mayan nobles who they presented to the king's son, Prince Philip. The nobles brought with them jars of beaten cocoa, mixed and ready to drink. They offered Philip his first taste of chocolate. He must have liked it because it quickly became a fashionable drink in the Spanish court.

THE SECRET DRINK

For decades, the Spanish kept chocolate a secret. They experimented with the new delicacy, adding cinnamon and vanilla to the sugar. They maintained the supply by planting cacao trees in their American colonies, forcing the natives to do the work of harvesting the pods and fermenting, drying, cleaning and roasting the seeds.

SPILLING THE BEANS

Eventually, in the late 1700s or early 1800s, chocolate spread to other parts of Europe. There are lots stories about how this happened. One legend claims some English pirates took chocolate from a Spanish ship and brought the drink to England. Another story is that Spanish monks mentioned it to some French monks. Or maybe the secret got out when Anne of Austria, daughter of King Philip III of Spain, gave King Louis XIII of France chocolate as a wedding gift when they married in 1615.

Anne of Austria, who became Queen of France, may have introduced chocolate to other parts of Europe.

14

GROWING POPULARITY

However it happened, a fashion for chocolate quickly spread through the royal courts and wealthy families of Europe. It was soon recognised as a nutritional, energy-rich beverage, and the Catholic Church allowed people to drink it during fasting periods as a substitute for food. Different ingredients were added, according to taste.

SERVING THE DRINK

Ornate china bowls were crafted to drink hot chocolate from. These were more than serving dishes – they became symbols of wealth and sophistication. In the 1640s, the Spanish developed the 'mancerina' – a plate with a recessed ring in the middle where a porcelain cup full of chocolate would sit. In the late 1600s, the French invented a metal pot for making chocolate. The pot had a hinged lid with a hole in it to hold the 'moussoir' – the French name for the molinillo (see page 13).

This engraving from around 1600 shows wealthy people drinking chocolate.

CHOCOLATE HOUSES

The first chocolate houses opened in London in 1657. These were places to enjoy a hot drink and discuss the issues of the day. They were visited by wealthy customers, and were furnished with fancy sofas, polished tables and valuable paintings on the walls.

DEATH BY CHOCOLATE

Pope Clement XIV was assassinated in 1774 when poison was added to his cup of drinking chocolate.

CHOCOLATE AND HEALTH

Chocolate is a fatty food, high in sugar and *calories*. It should therefore be eaten as an occasional treat as part of a balanced diet. Too much chocolate can lead to problems such as *obesity* and tooth decay. But does chocolate have any health benefits? According to research, dark chocolate, eaten in moderation, can help to reduce the risk of heart disease, lower blood pressure and possibly even reduce stress.

HEART DISEASE AND BLOOD PRESSURE

Cocoa contains a number of *nutrients*, including copper, zinc, iron, magnesium and fibre. It also contains beneficial substances called 'flavonols', which occur in a wide range of fruit and vegetables. Studies have shown that eating small amounts of dark chocolate, as part of a balanced diet, can reduce the risk of heart disease and can lower blood pressure. Most of the credit for this goes to the flavonols, which increase the flexibility of veins and arteries.

Chocolate is also less likely to cause heart problems because of the type of fat it contains. Cocoa butter contains a fat called 'stearic acid'. Unlike other fats, it is not known to raise *cholesterol* levels. High cholesterol can increase the risk of heart attack and stroke.

There is evidence that eating small amounts of dark chocolate can be healthy.

CHOCOLATE AS A MEDICINE

Cocoa has been used as a medicine for centuries, treating problems such as fever, stomach complaints, faintness, tiredness, or simply used as a drink to make other medicines taste better. In 1662, Spanish physician Juanes de Cardenas claimed that drinking it 'yields good nourishment to the body, it helps to digest ill humours, voiding the excrements by sweat and urine.'

Children under Dr Barnados enjoying chocolate.

DIABETES

Diabetes is a condition that causes a person's blood sugar level to become too high. Blood sugar levels are controlled by a *hormone* called *insulin*. One cause of diabetes is insulin resistance – when the body loses its resistance to insulin so it stops working properly. A 2008 Italian study showed that people who ate dark chocolate once a day for 15 days reduced their chance of insulin resistance by nearly 50 per cent.

STRESS

In a study carried out in 2009, 30 healthy people were given 40 g of dark chocolate a day for 14 days. They all experienced a reduction in stress hormones. However, the study, which was paid for by a major chocolate manufacturer, was small in scale and carried out over quite a short period of time. Further independent studies may be needed before we can be sure that chocolate can reduce stress.

THE PLANTATIONS

With the growing craze for chocolate among the European elite, the pressure was on to increase production. From the 17th century, cacao plantations spread through parts of the Americas along the equator, as the Portuguese, British and French, who all ruled countries in these areas, joined the Spanish in planting and harvesting the crop.

Clothing is being distributed to slaves on a cacao plantation.

SLAVERY

Millions of labourers were required to tend, harvest and process the cocoa. At first, the plantation owners forced captive local people to do this work. But huge numbers of the natives died from exhaustion or from European diseases that their bodies weren't used to, so slaves were imported from Africa to replace them.

GUAYAQUIL

When the Spanish arrived on the Guayaquil coast of Ecuador in the 1530s, they found wild forastero cacao growing. The beans were large, dry and bitter, but easy to grow and there were more than the criollo variety found in the Caribbean. They established cacao plantations and supplied cheap cocoa to the Spanish colonies of Mexico and Guatemala. Known as the 'cocoa of the poor', Guayaquil cocoa was looked down upon by the colonial elite.

VENEZUELA

The Spanish colony of Venezuela was the main *exporter* of cocoa to Europe during the 17th and 18th centuries. Venezuelan cocoa, known as 'caracas', was criollo, and greatly admired for its flavour. To meet demand, 20,000 African slaves were imported each year to work the plantations. In the 1620s, Dutch pirates seized some nearby islands and began trading with the Venezuelan planters. Because of this, a great deal of caracas ended up in Amsterdam rather than the Spanish port of Cadiz. The Spanish tried to stop the Dutch trade by patrolling the Venezuelan shoreline, but failed to stamp it out.

BRAZIL

Jesuit missionaries were the first to discover wild forastero cacao growing along the banks of the Amazon. They hired local natives to harvest the beans, which they shipped to Spain. It was not the tastiest cocoa, but nonetheless it generated a lucrative trade for the Jesuits until the 1740s when a series of epidemics virtually wiped out the native workforce. In 1759, the Jesuits were removed from Brazil by the new Portuguese governor, who started cacao plantations and brought in African slaves to work on them.

WEST INDIES

Slaves work on a cacao plantation in the West Indies.

The British captured Jamaica from the Spanish in 1655 and took over its criollo plantations, but these were wiped out by disease in the 1670s. French-owned Martinique and Guadeloupe then became the main cocoa producers, supplying the cocoa needs of France for most of the 1700s, replacing caracas. Another strong cacao island was Trinidad, seized by the British in 1802. After the criollo trees died out in 1727, some forastero seedlings were introduced. These accidentally bred with the surviving criollo to create a new species, trinitario, which combined the best qualities of both.

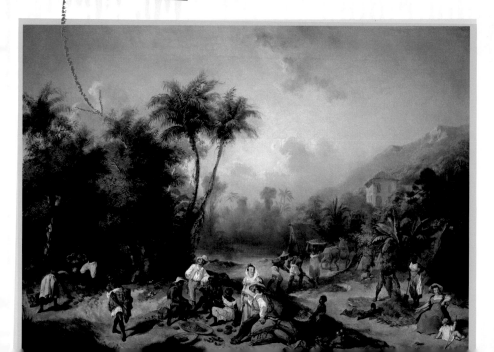

THE BIRTH OF AN INDUSTRY

Until the mid-18th century and the start of the Industrial Revolution in Europe, chocolate was mainly a handmade product. Time-consuming and expensive to produce, only the wealthy could afford it. The technological advances of the industrial age made it possible to produce lots of chocolate in a short space of time, and for the first time this tasty treat became available to the general public.

The Industrial Revolution introduced steam power to the chocolate-making process.

MECHANICAL MILLS

Traditionally, when the cocoa beans arrived from the Americas, they would have to be ground by hand. In 1732, a Frenchman named Dubuisson invented a charcoal-fired table that allowed cocoa to be ground more quickly and easily. By the 1770s, wind- and horse-powered mills began to appear. And in 1778, another Frenchman, Monsieur Doret, came up with a machine powered by *hydraulics* to grind the beans into liquor. However, it was a British *chocolatier*, Joseph Storrs Fry, who brought chocolate fully into the industrial age when he purchased a James Watt steam engine in 1789 to grind his cocoa beans.

WATER POWER

One of the earliest recorded examples of power machinery being used in chocolate manufacture occurred in the United States. In 1765, James Baker and John Hannon began making chocolate in Milton Lower Falls, Massachusetts. They rented space in an old water mill and used water power from the river to grind their cocoa beans. After Hannon was lost at sea in 1779, Baker went into business with his grandson Walter. The company still flourishes as the Walter Baker Company, and is the oldest chocolate manufacturer in the USA.

DUTCHING

In 1815, Dutch chemist and chocolatier Coenraad Johannes van Houten was trying to improve the flavour of his chocolate. He tried treating the liquor (the end product of the grinding process) with chemicals called 'alkaline salts' (sodium or potassium carbonate), and discovered that this allowed it to mix better with water and made the chocolate darker and milder. Some chocolate is still made today using this process, known as 'Dutching', and many people prefer 'Dutch' chocolate.

COCOA PRESS

Van Houten's most notable achievement came in 1828, with his invention of the cocoa press. This was a powerful hydraulic press that squeezed out the fat (cocoa butter) from the liquor. Until this time, the only way of separating out the fat was through a slow process of boiling and skimming. Van Houten's press managed to remove almost half the fat from the liquor. What remained was a cake that could be crushed into a powder, which became known as cocoa or cocoa powder. This new product made it much easier to make drinking chocolate. It also became the key ingredient in all future chocolate products.

Van Houten's invention paved the way for the chocolate bar.

THE ARRIVAL OF THE CHOCOLATE BAR

The world's first chocolate bar went on sale in 1847. It was produced by the Bristol-based chocolate manufacturer J.S. Fry & Sons in England, owned by Joseph Storrs Fry (see page 20). The Fry company had created their bar through a newly discovered process. In doing so they turned chocolate into a tasty, convenient snack that could be enjoyed by millions. Very soon, J.S. Fry & Sons were the biggest chocolate makers in the world!

A NEW PROCESS

To create their chocolate bars, Fry's made use of the recently discovered product, cocoa powder. They mixed a blend of cocoa powder and sugar with melted cocoa butter. By using cocoa butter instead of warm water as other manufacturers had been doing, they produced a thinner, less sticky paste that could be moulded. They named the resulting bar 'Chocolat Délicieux à Manger' ('Chocolate Delicious to Eat'), because French names were fashionable then. The key word was *Manger*, for this was the world's first successful eating chocolate.

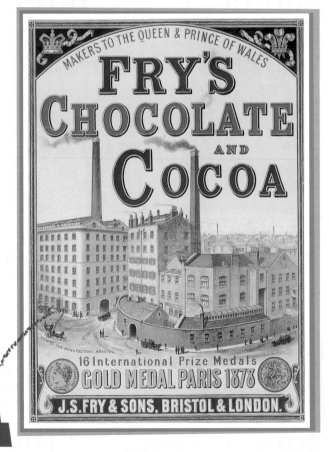

MAKERS TO THE QUEEN & PRINCE OF WALES

FRY'S CHOCOLATE AND COCOA

16 International Prize Medals
GOLD MEDAL PARIS 1878
J.S. FRY & SONS, BRISTOL & LONDON.

An 1880 advert for Fry's chocolate and cocoa.

RIVALRY

J.S. Fry & Sons became the world's biggest chocolate makers partly because they won the right to be the only supplier of chocolate to Britain's Royal Navy. The only manufacturer to rival them during the 19th century was Cadbury's. Founded in 1824, Cadbury's set themselves up as a major manufacturer in 1853 by becoming 'purveyors of chocolate to Queen Victoria'.

In 1866, Cadbury's launched a cocoa powder product, Cadbury's Cocoa Essence, which proved wildly popular. Fry's soon hit back with their own 'Cocoa Extract'. People began using cocoa powder not only to make drinking chocolate but also as an ingredient in homemade cakes and biscuits.

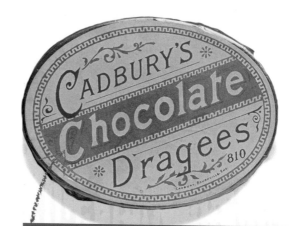

A box of chocolates from around 1900, which contained Cadbury's earliest Easter eggs.

CHOCOLATE BOX

In 1868, Cadbury's launched the world's first box of chocolates. They had used cocoa powder in liquid form to hand-coat a range of sweets. This opened up a whole new arena for chocolate products sold as gifts. It wasn't long before the first heart-shaped Valentine's Day chocolate boxes went on sale.

QUAKERS

The Cadbury family, like the Frys and the Rowntrees, another English chocolate-making family, belonged to a Christian movement called the Quakers. In keeping with their beliefs, they cared about workers' welfare. They built model towns and factories, such as Cadbury's Bournville near Birmingham. Fry's and Cadbury's also refused to buy cocoa from slave plantations.

SWISS CHOCOLATE

In 1819, François-Louis Cailler opened the first Swiss chocolate factory. In the decades that followed, the Swiss gradually acquired an international reputation as producers of high-quality chocolate. Swiss chocolate makers invented new methods that greatly improved the texture and smoothness of chocolate. Perhaps their most significant achievement was the invention of milk chocolate.

SUCHARD

Philippe Suchard, who was born in Boudry, Switzerland, became interested in chocolate-making at the age of 12. He opened his first factory in 1826, using a water-powered grinding mill. He invented the 'mélangeur' – a machine for mixing sugar and cocoa powder, which is still used today. By the end of the 19th century, his company was the biggest producer of Swiss chocolate and known throughout the world.

Henri Nestlé helped invent milk chocolate.

MILK CHOCOLATE

The Swiss were not the first people to mix milk with chocolate. That honour might belong to an Englishman, Nicholas Sanders, who produced a milky chocolate drink in 1727. However, it was the Swiss who first created milk chocolate in the solid form we know today.

It happened in two stages: first, Henri Nestlé, a Swiss chemist, made powdered milk through *evaporation*. Then a Swiss chocolatier named Daniel Peter used Nestlé's powder as an ingredient in his chocolate. In 1875, Peter and Nestlé teamed up to work and four years later they introduced the first milk chocolate bar. The smooth, creamy-tasting bar soon became one of most popular chocolate products available.

CONCHING

Another Swiss chocolatier, Rudolph Lindt, invented 'conching' (see page 9) in 1879. His conching machine was so named because its flat granite bed curved like a conch shell. Granite rollers would move back and forth, slapping against the curved ends of the bed and causing the chocolate liquor to splash over the rollers. This process caused friction and therefore heat to build up, breaking down the particles inside the liquor. Conching greatly improved both flavour and smoothness.

TEMPERING

In 1899, Swiss chocolatier Jean Tobler began selling 'Toblerone', the famous chocolate bar with the triangular cross-section. Tobler used a fine-quality chocolate, rich in cocoa butter. But he faced a problem – the cocoa butter would crystallise, causing the surface of the bar to become blotchy and grainy. The Swiss invention of tempering (see page 9) solved this.

The Swiss invented ways to make chocolate taste better than ever before.

FALL AND RISE OF AN INDUSTRY

Between 1890 and 1930, Swiss chocolate was at the height of its fame and popularity. People around the world admired the talents of the Swiss chocolatiers and the quality of their products. Then, in the 1930s, the Great Depression struck and the Swiss found it harder to export their chocolate. During World War II (1939–1945), there were restrictions on imports of sugar and cocoa. After the war, the industry revived and soon regained its global reputation. Today, most Swiss chocolate is eaten by the Swiss themselves. In fact, they have the highest rate of chocolate consumption per head of population in the world, with the average person eating 9 kg per year.

THE HENRY FORD OF CHOCOLATE MAKERS

On 13 September 1857, a boy was born in Pennsylvania, USA, who would grow up to be a serious rival to the great chocolate makers of Britain and Switzerland. Milton Snavely Hershey has been called 'the Henry Ford of Chocolate Makers', and he brought the same techniques of mass production to the chocolate industry that Ford, founder of the Ford Motor Company, brought to car making.

Hershey began as a maker of caramels.

EARLY LIFE

At the age of 14, Hershey was apprenticed to a confectioner, and five years later he started his own confectionary-making business. In 1893, Hershey visited an exhibition in Chicago where he saw a chocolate-making machine in operation. It was a revelation. He bought the machine and started using it to make chocolate coatings for his caramels. Soon afterwards, he sold his caramel business and used the money to build himself a chocolate factory.

THE HERSHEY BAR

In the 1890s, milk chocolate was still a luxury treat. Hershey was determined to make it available to all. In 1899, after years of experimenting, he developed a successful formula. The Hershey Bar – the first American milk chocolate bar – went on sale in 1900. In 1907, Hershey made Hershey's Kisses – bite-sized drops of milk chocolate, each wrapped in silver foil – which were a huge hit. The next year, he released the almond Hershey Bar.

THE TOWN OF HERSHEY

Hershey's factory soon grew into a town for his workers, far bigger than anything Cadbury or Rowntree built. The town of Hershey was dominated by the factory and the owner's huge mansion. There was also a Hershey Department Store, Hershey Bank, Hershey Park and Hershey Hotel. There were schools, churches, libraries, clubs, even a zoo and a roller-coaster.

Milk for the factory was supplied by the dairy farms that Hershey owned. He established another town of Hershey in Cuba, with five sugar mills, to supply the factory's sugar, and he even built a 400-km railway to transport the sugar to the shipping port. By the 1920s, it was producing 23,000 kg of cocoa each day.

Hershey died in 1945, aged 88, but his business continues to thrive. Today it remains North America's largest chocolate producer with 40 per cent of the market, and it sells its products in 50 countries.

THE RATION D BAR

During World War II, the US Army asked Hershey to produce a chocolate bar for their troops' rations.

Their requirements were as follows.
The bar must:
- weigh around 113 g
- not melt at high temperatures
- be high in calories
- not taste so good that troops would crave it.

Hershey came up with the Ration D bar.

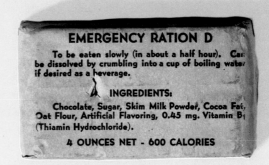

EMERGENCY RATION D

To be eaten slowly (in about a half hour). Can be dissolved by crumbling into a cup of boiling water if desired as a beverage.

INGREDIENTS:
Chocolate, Sugar, Skim Milk Powder, Cocoa Fat, Oat Flour, Artificial Flavoring, 0.45 mg. Vitamin B₁ (Thiamin Hydrochloride).

4 OUNCES NET - 600 CALORIES

It was so successful that by 1945 the company was producing 24 million bars a week.

CHOCOLATE TODAY

Today, chocolate is one of the most popular foods and flavours in the world. It's used in a vast number of sweet foods from Easter eggs to chocolate chip cookies. It's even found its way into popular culture with books and films like *Charlie and the Chocolate Factory* and *Chocolat*. There are around 3.8 million tonnes of chocolate made each year, and demand keeps rising.

WHERE IS IT GROWN?

Because the global demand for chocolate is so great, cocoa crops have spread beyond the Americas to other tropical regions. Today, the biggest cocoa-producing countries are Ghana, Nigeria and the Ivory Coast in West Africa. Other important producers are Brazil and Ecuador in South America, and Malaysia and Indonesia in Southeast Asia. Approximately two-thirds of the world's cocoa is produced in West Africa, and around 40 per cent comes from the Ivory Coast.

Since 1875, it has become a tradition at Easter to eat chocolate eggs.

COCOA FARMS

Turning cocoa beans into chocolate is now done by machines, but cocoa is still grown and harvested by hand, mainly because the cacao trees need carefully looking after. The colonial plantations that once supplied the world with cocoa are all gone. A few companies still own their own farms, but most cocoa is grown on small, family-owned farms.

CHALLENGES

The price that manufacturers pay for cocoa goes up and down, depending on the global economy and what is happening on the world's *stock exchanges*. Low prices can push farmers into poverty. They are also vulnerable to bad weather and tree diseases. One disease, Black Pod, is killing one in 10 cacao trees worldwide and causing a drop in yield of 20–30 per cent. However, in times of need, the shade tree crops – the trees that give the cacao trees their shade – can provide a back-up source of income. Shade tree crops can produce, for example, timber, fruit, fibre, rubber, honey and resin.

Workers spread out cocoa beans to dry.

ASSISTANCE

Farmers receive assistance from the World Cocoa Foundation (WCF), an organisation of chocolate manufacturers. Their stated aim is to help farmers develop sustainable growing methods to grow a better-quality crop. Together with the Bill and Melinda Gates Foundation, the WCF claim to have helped 165,000 cocoa-farming families increase their income. The program also supports better nutrition, healthcare and children's education for the families.

COCOA CRAVINGS

Cocoa, first sipped as a bitter drink by Mesoamericans thousands of years ago, has in the past few centuries become something desired by millions across the world. It has taken on forms that the Olmecs, Mayas and Aztecs could not have dreamed of, and our appetite for chocolate shows no sign of getting smaller.

HOW MUCH CHOCOLATE DO WE EAT?

The average adult eats between 5 and 9.5 kg of chocolate per year, which means it would take them only 10 years or so to eat their entire bodyweight in chocolate.

TIMELINE

c. 1900 BCE	The first evidence of chocolate being eaten in Mesoamerica.
1600–100 BCE	The Olmecs grow cocoa beans.
c. CE 600	The Maya establish cocoa plantations in the Yucatan.
1300s	Chocolate becomes popular with the Aztec nobles. They begin exacting it as tribute from conquered peoples.
1502	Christopher Columbus and his fellow sailors discover cocoa beans for the first time.
1521	The Spanish conquistadors defeat the Aztecs and inherit their cocoa supply.
1544	Maya nobles introduce Prince Philip of Spain to chocolate. It becomes a fashionable drink in the Spanish court.
1590	Spanish nuns in Oaxaca, Mexico, sweeten chocolate with honey, cinnamon and sugar, greatly increasing its appeal.
1631	The Spanish doctor Antonio Colmenero de Ledesma publishes the first recipe for chocolate.
1641	The scientist Johann Voldkammer introduces chocolate to the Germans.
1657	The first chocolate house opens in London.
1659	A baker, David Chaillou, becomes France's first chocolatier.
1732	French inventor Monsieur Dubuisson invents a heated table for grinding cocoa beans.
1789	Joseph Storrs Fry is the first chocolate maker to use a steam engine to grind cocoa.
1828	Coenraad van Houten invents the cocoa press, creating cocoa powder.
1847	J.S. Fry & Sons create the chocolate bar, the first successful eating chocolate.
1868	Cadbury's release the world's first box of chocolates.
1879	The Swiss chocolatiers Daniel Peter and Henri Nestlé invent milk chocolate.
1879	Rudolph Lindt invents conching.
1900	Milton Hershey sells the first Hershey Bar, using mass-production methods to make chocolate affordable to ordinary people.
1912	Belgian chocolatier Jean Neuhaus invents a chocolate shell that can be filled with soft centres and nut pastes.
1930	The Swiss company Nestlé make the first white chocolate, named Galak (Milky Bar in the UK).
2005	Cadbury's buys Green & Black's, a manufacturer of organic chocolate. Organic chocolate is made without the use of artificial pesticides and chemical fertilisers.

GLOSSARY

calorie A unit of energy.

chocolatier A person who makes or sells chocolate.

cholesterol A substance found in most body tissues. High concentrations of cholesterol in the blood can lead to disease of the arteries.

colonies Countries controlled by another country.

conquistador One of the Spanish conquerors of Mexico and Peru in the 16th century.

crystallisation Formation into crystals – solid substances consisting of atoms or molecules arranged in a geometrically regular form.

equator An imaginary line drawn around the middle of the Earth, spaced equally between the North Pole and South Pole.

evaporate to turn a liquid into a gas.

export To send goods abroad to sell them.

ferment To break down chemically by the action of bacteria or other microorganisms.

hormone A substance produced by humans and other organisms to stimulate particular cells or tissues into action.

hybrid The offspring of two plants (or animals) of different species or varieties.

hydraulic Power transmitted by the controlled circulation of pressurised liquid.

import To bring goods into a country from abroad to sell them.

Industrial Revolution The rapid development of industry that began in Britain in the 18th and 19th centuries, brought about by the introduction of steam power and the growth of factories.

insulin A hormone that lowers the levels of a type of sugar called 'glucose' in the blood.

Jesuit missionary A member of the Society of Jesus, a Roman Catholic group of priests, who go on trips to promote their religion.

machete A broad, heavy knife.

Mesoamerica The region of Central America where a several different groups of people lived before the Spanish arrived in the 15th and 16th centuries.

nutrient A substance that provides nourishment necessary for life and growth.

obesity A state of being very fat or overweight that is harmful to your health.

plantation An estate or large farm where a crop such as cocoa, coffee or sugar is grown.

residue A small amount of something that remains after the main part has gone.

stock exchange A market in which stocks (shares in companies) are bought and sold.

tribute A regular payment made by a conquered state to its conquerors.

FURTHER INFORMATION

Books

The Biography of Chocolate (How Did That Get There?) by Adrianna Morganelli (CRABTREE, 2006)

A Chocolate Bar (How It's Made) by Sarah Ridley (FRANKLIN WATTS, 2009)

The Mars Family (Food Dudes) by Joanne Mattern (CHECKERBOARD BOOKS, 2011)

Explore! Chocolate by Liz Gogerly (WAYLAND, 2014)

Who Was Milton Hershey by James Buckley Jr (PUTNAM, 2015)

Websites

www.thestoryofchocolate.com/

https://blog.udemy.com/history-of-chocolate-for-kids/

http://facts-about-chocolate.com/chocolate-history/

www.fairtrade.org.uk/en/farmers-and-workers/cocoa/about-cocoa

http://worldcocoafoundation.org/

www.info-galaxy.com/Chocolate/History/history.html

INDEX

THE STORY OF FOOD

TITLES IN THE SERIES

ISBN: 9780750296618

What is Tea?
The Production Process
The Birth of Tea
The Japanese Tea Ceremony
Tea Comes to Europe
Is Tea Healthy?
The Tea Trade
Taxes and Smuggling
The Boston Tea Party
Customs and Rituals
Tea Clippers
The Tea Bag
The Modern World

ISBN: 9780750296595

What is Chocolate?
Cacao Farming
From Beans to Chocolate
The Origins of Chocolate
The Spanish Discover
  Chocolate
Chocolate and Health
Chocolate Comes to Europe
The Plantations
The Birth of an Industry
The Arrival of the
  Chocolate Bar
Swiss Chocolate
The Henry Ford of
  Chocolate Makers
Chocolate Today

ISBN: 9780750296601

What is Sugar?
How is Sugar Used?
Sugarcane
Sugar Beet
Ancient Times
Sugar and Our Health
The Middle Ages
Sugarcane and the Americas
Sugar and Slavery
Sugar Beet in Europe
An Ever Sweeter World
The Changing Industry
Sugar Today

ISBN: 9780750296588

What is Salt?
Salt for Seasoning
How is Salt Produced?
Salt for Preserving Food
Salt in the Ancient World
Salt and Our Health
Salt in Religion
Salt in the Middle Ages
Exploring the New World
Salt Wars
Salt in Early America
The Salt March
Salt in Today's World

WAYLAND
www.waylandbooks.co.uk